AF455224

The List

JENNIFER SHAW

ISBN 978-0-359-73607-2 90000

2019 Lulu Author.

ID:24859533

www.lulu.com

The List

The List is a book of Poetry about abused women. The poems in this book show the different kinds of abuse that women have encountered. The final poem in this book is alternate ways to take control of a situation!!!

I began writing this book during an abusive marriage... Through a counseling class where I shared with many others that had experienced abuse... Sharing their stories... helped me share my own and to share our experiences through poetry!!! I wanted to discuss the issues in this book that they are not able to discuss themselves. Poetry can be happy, sad, and informative, expressive, and a part of healing!!! It can also be a safety net!!!

Everyone Gets Angry...

It's What You Do After You Get Angry...

That Makes The Difference!!!

Table of Contents

One Million

He starts from the top
He works his way down slow
Calling each one by name
So everyone will know…
He wants to hurt her feelings
He wants her to feel it in her heart
He watches and waits for his words
To tear her apart…
He wants her to feel it
With every stroke of his tongue
The words that he yells
Are like the fists he once flung…
She knew everyone could see
The bruises on her jaws
But he never stops
Even when he has pointed out…
One Million Flaws!!!
He just seems to gain strength
With every tear she's cried
Each word cut a little deeper
As she hurts more inside…
His physical strength wasn't enough
Or the bruises that his fists left
He appeared to get more joy
Watching her die inside herself…
Now each morning she look in the mirror
She sees the bruises on her jaws
And she still remembers
Him calling out…

One Million Flaws!

She couldn't understand
Why he wouldn't just walk away
And allow her some peace
She would have still struggled everyday…
The losing of her confidence
The bruises and the pain
Now tells the stories
And none of them are the same…
Memories that make her cry
And the words that are hard to say
She struggles to find her strength
Though it becomes a little easier everyday…
Hurting her gave him joy
It made him feel like a man
But since they took him away
She's finding the strength to stand…
She turned down every mirror
You can see as you walk through her halls
Because all she sees when she looks in them
Is him yelling out…
One Million Flaws!
He wanted to scar her life
To she would live alone
He wanted to take away her happiness
To make her think she wasn't strong…
The first time took her by surprise
Because she had never expected this
The days she covered up his actions
Has now put their lives at risk…

So many people knew her situation

But no one wanted to get involved

She stayed longer than she should have

But safety was the most important issue for her to resolve...

Some days were very bad

But there were worse days now

She just focused on protecting her children

So she would survive somehow...

She had always been a strong woman

But those bruises he left on her jaws

Reminded her of the hours crouched in corners

And him yelling out...

One Million Flaws!

The key is to forget

Which is easier said than done

Taking care of herself and her children

And not having to pack up her things and run...

Her children were the reason she found her strength

She has never viewed herself the same

She learned to fight back her tears

And not hold her head down in shame...

The next man would share her burden

He would have to be strong

He would need to treat her gentle

And promise not to do her wrong...

He would easily see the bruises

But he would never ask her to recall

The memory of this person

That found on her...

One Million Flaws!

She'll live with the memories

And the scars don't seem to decrease

But the strength and confidence inside her

Is beginning to find some release…

The way he acted was horrible

But through it all she's still alive

He thought he had broken her will

Yet she found the strength to survive…

The pain is devastating

Sometimes it causes her to stumble or fall

But her worst memory is him standing there

Yelling out…

ONE MILLION FLAWS!

I Couldn't Tell

You were sexy
Your eyes like pearls
You swept me off my feet
I thought I was living in a perfect world...
A gift that caught my eye
Words that blew my mind
I was bragging to my friends
About you all the time...
You said you loved me
It was love at first sight
Then something happened to you
Late one night...
I came in a little late
Maybe you were talking to your friends
You started hitting me
When I walked in...
When I first met you
I couldn't tell
That you would change once you got me
Or that life with you would be a living hell!!!
I didn't know you wanted control
I didn't know you would boss me around
I didn't expect to be cut
I didn't expect to be kicked or slapped down...
I had no idea you were a fighter
Or that you would cause me so much pain
I didn't expect to be talked down to
Or called out of my name...
I have no answer

I still can't say why?
My family liked you
And you pretended to be the perfect guy...

To this day I can't understand

I could never be so wise

I could not tell

That you would change before my eyes...

Now I'm shunning my friends

Because I'm broken, bruised, and ashamed

My face is hidden beneath make up and dark shades

And I'm still wondering why you changed...

The day you walked in to my life

I thought destiny had sent me someone great

But these few years we have been together

I've realized that this wasn't fate...

God was trying to tell me

But His voice I did not hear

And until I gathered my courage and left

I wasn't thinking clear...

Now as I think about it

What happened to me each day

I realize that it wasn't my fault

I didn't make you act that way...

You never knew how to show love

I can tell by the bruises you left

And after all I went through with you

I still Love myself!!!

At first all I could see was your looks

You looked like the perfect male

But it turned out that you were a sick little boy...

And I Couldn't Tell!

Physical Hits; Emotional Bruises

Like a knife cutting through your skin
Fists of fury like a fiery wind
Heavy as steel on the ground
That's the way anger comes around…
Black and blue as the marks they leave behind
Remains the echo of all those words that was so unkind
Physical hits will go away
Emotional bruises seem to stay…
Hands smashing; tongues lashing against a solid wall
Cracks forming; hearts crumbling as your self- esteem start to fall
Eyes swollen; black and blue against your skin
Fear rising; his voice patronizing as he comes walking in
Trying to be strong or at least doing your best
While someone that claimed to love you put you through this mess…
Physical hits will go away
Emotional bruises seem to stay…
Now there you sit with a tear stained face once more
Hugging yourself shaking in a corner on the floor
Wondering what happened to that person you thought you knew
His voice shouting like a bass drum; "it's because of you…"
Not knowing how to end it… being too afraid to try
Seeing the rage… feeling the pain as his fists swing by
Physical hits will go away
Emotional bruises seem to stay…
Waking up with hands around your neck
Your first thought… what the heck?
Tears streaming from your eyes
Fighting; fading into unconsciousness as you slowly realize…
Mistakes were made that you can't correct

Faith was shattered that you can't resurrect

Fists powered by anger... words like sharpened darts

Piercing through a strong mind... breaking a wounded heart

Physical hits will go away

Emotional bruises seem to stay...

Now that the trauma has passed

You think the memories are done

Just as you try to live again

You're haunted by every single one...

Waking up from your sleep in a cold sweat

Shaking uncontrollably because your clothes are soaking wet

Fear grasp your emotions... horrible thoughts come your way

No one knows what you had to live through everyday...

Life leaves you broken... wondering will anyone ever understand

Your wounds... your broken heart was never part of your plan

It's hard to forget the holes left behind

People say everything heals in time...

Physical Hits Go Away

Emotional Bruises Seem To Stay!

Broken

I came to you broken
Where my heart had grown cold
Cause of all the bruises and wounds
It has had to hold
I know they are there
Even though you don't see
Trying to take away my hope
While squeezing more tears out of me
I never had anyone to make me feel like they loved me
Or even make me feel like I belonged
I haven't had anyone to stroke my hair
Or make me feel strong
I've always had my heart broken
Until I felt so messed up inside
But I was always determined to succeed
No matter how much I cried
I've been pushed and I've been shaken
I've been tricked and sometimes I was mistaken
But the words I have spoken to ease my pain
Kept me from being broken
And holding my head down in shame

Between Happening and Had

Laughing and yelling
Mean words and things were said
Frowns and tears
Hurtful memories going through my head
Now you're wondering why I'm always sad
It's because all great things are
Between happening and had!!!
It so happens… that a friendship was broken
Love was lost
Children suffered…
There was emotional cost
I was hurt
Dirty words were said
You threw things and I got mad
That proved that everything breaks
Between happening and had!!!
The sky was cloudy
Rain begin to fall
There was so much you didn't believe
For you tomorrow never came at all
But I packed my bags cause…
It was time for me to leave
My dreams weren't important to you
But you couldn't understand why I was sad
We never talked, we never touched
So I sealed my heart in a bag
Everything broke…
Between happening and had!!!

I couldn't make you listen

You said, "you did nothing to me

That meant everything was gone

So many years of pain

Since you done nothing

Nothing could be done right or wrong

Well, that was too bad

Because everything ended

Between Happening and Had!!!

Painful Love

I met a girl who told me about something I never heard
She called it painful love
I said, "it's not in God's word"
I asked her what's painful love
Tell me how it's been
She said, "it happens with my boyfriend time and time again"

She said, "he hits me, kicks me, and slam me against the wall"
When my body is covered with blood and bruises
He stands and watch me stagger and fall
Then he says: I love you
You make me act this way
I'm sorry that you are hurt
But you made me hit you yesterday
He calls it painful love that we share
He grabs me and hug me
And say, if he didn't hit me how would I know he care...
Her eyes were black and swollen nearly tight
I asked her what happened
She said, "he hits me every night"
Her ribs were bandaged
She could hardly stand
She said, "he didn't mean it"
He loves me... "I can tell by the way he holds my hand"

She called it painful love
I said, "you should leave"

Stop this hurt now
Forget about this man
God will show you how
She said, "things will get better wait and see"
As I walked out the door I knew that it wouldn't be

The next day I got a call
I didn't know what to say
I sat on my bed and cried
I didn't want it to end that way
The police said, "he beat her and hit her in the head"
"before she hit the floor ... she was already dead"

I prayed a prayer for her lost soul
Then I read from the bible
I wished she had taken control
I told her not to stay
There is nothing such as painful love
I watched as the police took him away

Many tears fell as they lay her in the ground
I remember her saying, "things would change one day"
She shouldn't have waited for things to turn around
She lost her life because she thought that way

Don't talk about painful love
Love that's painful can never be true
Don't listen to anyone who talks like that
That's a person's way to keep using abuse on you

Beat Down

Beat down by life
Twisted by fate
Pushed over until
There was no more she could take

A broken heart
A tormented soul
Loss in a time
That no one knows

Betrayed by love
Not knowing who you can trust anymore
Wanting to start again
Yet fighting the feelings that you felt before

Wishing for something great
Looking for something that will take your breath away
Living for your own happiness
Hoping things will get better someday

Beat down by life
Touched by fate
Changing your situation
Into something great

A heart that needs healing
A spirit that's broken no more

An amazing turn of events

To make you feel something like you never felt before

Weakened

The sadness in my soul

Pours down like rain

As my heart opens

And pours out its pain...

The disbelief in my mind

Scrambles like broken glass

As my mouth opens

To speak of a painful past...

The tears in my eyes

Blur my sight

As I try not to cry

In the middle of the night...

I have learned to listen

As my heart speaks aloud

Because the silence was deafening

As it drowned out the crowd...

To lose myself

Means I'll have to fall

How sad it is

To leave it all...

The hurt in my life

Has been steady like the rivers flow

Circumstance has pushed me around

And like a withered flower I grow…

My mind paints a picture

Of so many things gone wrong

While my eyes open

To reveal a woman determined to stay strong…

The wounds in my soul

Strengthens my words

While I open my heart

To tell you things you never heard…

My soul, my heart, my mind, my eyes

Open a window and a door

To a beaten down, weakened woman

You won't find in me anymore!!!

The Road

We each travelled down a road
To get where we are today
We were stomped, hit, and knocked down
We were treated any kind of way...
We were yelled at
We were talked to like we didn't matter
We were controlled by angry fists
We were not aware of anything better...
We were born in a time
When no one was seeking change
When anger behind closed doors
Wasn't called Domestic Violence by name...
We each travelled down a road
To get where we are today
We were slapped, punched, and kicked down
We were treated any kind of way...
Some of us it took by surprise
Some of us was more aware
Some of us has already lived through
This same horrible kind of affair...
We were shocked, we were astonished, we were dismayed
We were overtaken by fear
We fought, we hid, we ran away
Now we are thankful we're still here...
We each travelled down a road
To get where we are today

We were beat, choked, and slammed against walls

We were treated any kind of way…

We had stumbled down

We were sinking in despair

We found our strength somehow

We knew we couldn't stay there…

We searched for courage

So we could begin

We walked through fire

Wondering if we could live again…

We each travelled down a road

To get where we are today

We were stomped, hit, and knocked down

We were treated any kind of way…

But we stood up

To find our unbroken dreams

We had to push pass doubt

It took more strength it seems…

It was a struggle

That some will never know

But the hardest part is

Letting those bad memories go…

We each travelled down a road

To get where our dreams could be realized

We had to struggle, hold on, and get off the ground

And through it all we survived!!!

Abused

He told her he loved her

But he kicked her with steel toe shoes

He beat her with his fists

He felt like he had nothing to lose...

She fought back while she cried

He just got angrier

Then he punched her in her eyes...

He stared out the window

Whenever she was gone

Telling himself she was with another man

And

That he would get her when she got home...

He said, "I Love you"

When he hugged her tight

But he stomped her and kicked her

After the children went to bed that night...

She would never tell

Her horrible unseen glory

But everyone around her knew

Because her face and arms told the story...

She wasn't aware of the danger

He had done this so many times before

Kicking and beating his first wife

Watching as she lay bleeding on their kitchen floor...

Today she said she would leave

Later he would change her mind

But something will make him angry again

Then he will start punching her one…more…time…

Fists filled with anger

Words that always hurt

Yelling and screaming at her

Treating her like dirt…

But this time something snapped inside

He couldn't run because she blocked the door

But he could see it in her eyes

As he slowly fell to the floor…

A night to the heart

Blood leaking out

He started to see black

While the words came from her mouth…

The police were called

The ambulance came

He arrived at the hospital

The doctor said, "it's a shame…"

His life was saved

The relationship was through

She'd had enough

The nurse said, "she won't take anymore from you…"

She carries the scars of all she of her past pain

Cuts and bruises that will never heal

A badly hurt leg that causes her to limp

A reminder that her tragedy was real!

Get the Message

You didn't want me when you had me
You said, I wasn't good enough
So… I moved on in another direction
Because I got tired of hearing that stuff
Now it seems harder for you for some reason
To let me go and say we're through
I'm trying to make my life better
But
You keep trying to make me want you
I lost so much time while we were together
Trying to fix what you said was wrong
I know I'm not perfect in anyway
But
It was you I should have left alone

Fists of fury
Words as angry as hell
Left me in tears for 15 years
I don't know why it was so hard to tell
No matter how many times I stress this
You keep trying to back track into my life
But
I'm gonna need for you to get the message!!!

My heart never pounded
My hands never sweat
I should've known you weren't the one
And
Now I wouldn't have this to regret

I can't say I have fond memories
Because that would just be a bunch of lies
Those good times you claim you remember
You were seeing through someone else's eyes

I just hope that the children know
That what you were showing was never love
And
The way you were acting all these years
Was never what I was dreaming of!
Now... I don't know why it was so hard for you
No matter how many times I stress this
I'm Gonna Need for You to Get This Message
You are the reason people call them Exes!!!

For 15 Years

15 years I looked in a mirror into the eyes of a stranger

I saw someone I never knew

Suddenly I began to realize

That I couldn't spend all my life with you

You turned me into a person that couldn't smile at herself

You being angry at me all the time

Not knowing who I was

Because a lot of me was hiding in my mind

15 years I looked in a mirror

At someone I didn't want to see

Suddenly I realized

That I didn't know me

I had changed the things that mattered

Trying to please everyone else

But there was one person that wasn't happy

I wasn't happy with myself!!!

15 years I looked in a mirror

But behind my eyes I saw you

Seeing a stranger behind my eyes

Let me know what I had to do

Well, I couldn't seem to make you understand

That had been someone else

But all I wanted

Was to start being myself

15 years I looked in a mirror
And saw another face its true
Not wanting to change my values
I begin to slowly open myself up to you

You acted like what I said didn't matter
You even called me a stupid fool
I quickly said you are right
I'm a fool for staying with you

15 years I looked in a mirror
Yesterday it shattered while I was standing there
Quickly I realized it was a sign
Letting me know that I was unaware

15 years I looked in a mirror
I saw someone else looking back at me
I didn't have the strength to decide what to do
That person wasn't who I wanted to see

15 years I looked in a mirror
That had me standing on the outside of my life looking in
Now I'm looking through my own eyes
This is when life begins!!!

15 years I looked in a mirror...

The Attack

She was pushed

Then shoved to the ground

She struggled to get away

It wasn't enough… the strength that she found

He ripped her clothes in the brawl

He even wounded her heart

The knife wasn't used at all

When it was over… she laid there and cried

She wished she had died

Taken to the hospital

She wasn't bruised enough

The police started asking her questions

Some of them were tough

Sitting in court because she wouldn't run

The lawyer started his theory

The hurt wasn't done

The trail was over

He only received a few weeks for his crime

She was in despair

They didn't seem to care

He planned to return to her house

He stocked her for weeks

It became too much pressure with no rest

She cried continuously

She was in distress

That night he lost something

It was a long road

The hurt and pain was still strong

The trauma would last forever

She was left alone

It was during the second attack

She screamed and cried

He stumbled and fell

There he laid and died

No one to break her heart anymore

She was no longer in distress

Her life would never be like before

Stop The Silence

There she stood with circles around her eyes
Where tears had formed and dried
Looking like a raccoon's face
In her own silent place…
Where she had been hit many times before
While you listened behind a closed door
Where each night her pain begins
While you slept peacefully until your night ends…
She became a number on a page
While she was beat out of rage
A static in her own right
In and out of sight
To make her world seem black
He took an iron and burnt her back…
While tears ran down her face
She watched the handcuffs as he left her place
Her swollen eyes
Couldn't tell any lies
The horrible memories made it easier for her to do
But
He changed his identity and moved in with you…
Now all her burdens are yours to hold
So… you don't have to endure the stories she told
As he left his hands cuffed behind
He promised her that he would be kind…
With her head hanging
The gavel banging
She looked through her hair
Sitting on the stand in that cold chair

She testified about what he had done

Her good-bye was… The Final One!!!

A World Without Mirrors

In the darkness
Where the shadows hide as well
Bruises don't show at all
And
Pain can't speak or tell…
Cries are muffled
Words without sound
Hands to small to fight
Tears streaming down

A world without mirrors
Means no one can see
How things happened
Or how things will be…
A lost happiness
Innocence stolen away
Someone lost forever
Someone died that day…
A struggle to survive in a world
You could no longer understand
Moving through life with challenges
More than a normal life demand

A world without mirrors
Shows no pain
Because faces are hidden
When people are ashamed…
Survival is a blessing
sometimes it doesn't seem that way

But

Learning to love you again

Is harder than anyone can say…

Forgotten events leave scars

But sometimes they don't show

Years go by without words

And

Other people never know

Your life seems to end…

The years grew harder

Because a soul was torn

By words that raised questions

Of a child that was forever scorn…

A world without mirrors

A world without cries

A world that hides the truth

Is a world that covers lies!

Imprisoned

Imprisoned in a world that leave no room

For happiness or joy

Figuring out how to escape the ultimate doom...

Like a jail I see through the bars

Shielding myself from the Son's light

Hiding my hideous scars...

Burning like a raging fire from words so mean

Being cut as if with a thousand knives

Not knowing these scars cannot be seen...

Keeping everything in mind

While my world crumbles inside

But allowing my pain to define...

My Life

So... long living through the unkind

Waiting and wishing to be rescued

Because of the piece I cannot find...

Pretending that everything is going great you see

Running from the face in the mirror

Finding out that person is me...

Having being pushed to the edge

Not knowing our own strength

Rescuing myself from the ledge...

He pretended to be kind

Hoping I would lose my balance

Thinking I had sacrificed my mind...

Imprisoned by a heart that you gave with love so true

Shattered and kicked around with no concern

Before it was thrown back at you...

Like a thick broken glass

I looked through my eyes in shame

Like a movie playing watching my past…

Imprisoned in my flesh yet always looking out

Being hit with words and sometimes fists

Wondering what life was all about…

Gathering my piece of mind that’s left

Finding a stronger me

Helping others as well as myself…

Realizing that my strength was always inside

Getting power from the wind

Blowing down the fear we call pride…

Trying to reach the light in the distance

Being hindered by memories

Not knowing how to dismiss them…

Imprisoned by the scars that only we can see

Being led to believe they are visible

Because that’s how he wanted it to be…

We must break down the walls that distort our vision

We are not fat, ugly, or sickening

So… we must move pass our indecision…

Imprisoned yet… No more to lose

Now standing up to prove it to yourself

This is what I chose…

We were shadowed

We were stalked

We were abused

Now we laugh

Now we share

NOW we are whatever…

WE CHOOSE!!!

Invisible

People pass me on the street

They don't even smile or speak

They act like they don't see me

I wear scarves on my head

And

My clothes a little big

It all hides me from the world I'm in

I'm invisible to them

They don't see my eyes as they shine

Taking in wonders of every kind

They have other things on their mind

I don't talk very loud

I usually wear a smile

I stay just outside the crowd

I'm invisible no doubt

Since I was very small

Seems no one could see me at all

This is the childhood I recall

Most days I don't go anywhere

When I do it's like I'm not even there

So… I try to stay in the fresh air

I'm invisible so no one even stare

Sometimes I go to dinner and get a plate

Just for my order I must sit and wait
They forget I'm there because I don't have a date

I laugh and joke to my friends
About this big world I'm in
Where I sit with my pen
I'm invisible then

They tell me to calm down
Whenever I come around
Because there's no humor found
In the way my stories sound

So… most times I sit alone
I sing and play songs
That helps me stay strong
I'm invisible to them… am I wrong?

I don't have a problem with any of this
It's given my life a new twist
It keeps me taking risk
While others wonder what they've missed

I'm full of words to say
That no one has heard from me anyway
That I write from day to day
I'm invisible to them… ok

People want me to feel intimated
That sometimes make me frustrated

Even though it's never stated

I'm invisible… I guess invisibility is overrated

I move through this world slow

No one even know

Where I attempt to go

I'm invisible… it never shows

Someday I'll take a chance no doubt

I'll be the one people say good things about

The things I do will stand out

Then I won't be invisible…that's what the world will shout

So… be careful how you treat

The people you never meet

The ones you pass on the street

Those you choose not to greet

I'm invisible… but it's not defeat

I've been in this world so long

That nothing seems to go wrong

That can keep me from holding on

I try to find ways to stay strong

But when I hear people criticize

I realize they would be surprised

At the bruises I hide from when I was brutalized

I'm invisible… for that I do not apologize

I'm invisible to a world of people that's unaware

Of how hard it is to care

When unkind people whisper and stare

Because they have not been there

People pass me on the street

They don't even speak

I'm the person that they don't see

I'M INVISIBLE!

I'm Saying Good-bye For The Last Time

You keep saying you're sorry
You keep saying give you another chance
I don't know what to tell you
But… I'm tired of this same ole dance

You broke my heart
You called me names
But… now you want me to listen
While you convinced me you would change

I trusted you once
But… I won't believe you again
Because trusting you twice
Means living this lie that will never end

Our girls are watching me
And
The women down the street
Some of the girls don't understand
Why yesterday Mrs. J got beat…

You always said, "I wouldn't become anything"
You said, "everything I tried would fall through"
So… I'm picking up my children
And
Saying good-bye to the likes of you

I'm saying good-bye for the last time

This won't happen again
Because if I don't say good-bye
This will never end

My boys can't understand
Why I put up with you this long
I was the one that always took a stand
I was the one... they had only saw me be strong

Now I'm taking back my strength
I'm starting out brand new
I'm gonna live my life like God ordained
Because it's been so long since I got over you

So... you won't see me hiding anymore
You won't see me crouched down in fear
I'm saying good-bye for the last time
And
I hope you heard it loud and clear

People are saying good-byes are not forever
But... that's not the case with mine
You won't have us to kick around anymore
Because I'm saying... Good-Bye For The Last
TIME!

Meltdowns

Doors slamming

Windows shake

People yelling

Hearts break

Women afraid for their children

Children trying to take a stand

Women jumping in the middle

Of their child and a large angry man

A meltdown is coming

But… the emotional hits won't let her rise

Angry hands break things

Her voice can't be heard through painful cries

Loud voices

Punches passed

A child stands up

This future won't last

Tears are shed

Bruises are made

A mother takes a stand

A foundation is laid

A meltdown is happening again

The reason is unclear

Names are called

Memories ripped away… that was held dear

Family ties are loosened

Hearts are broken in two

A family's values are pushed aside

Not a good thing to do

Blood was spilled

No apologies were made

A foundation cracked

Because of the hits that were gave

The meltdown is over

But… just for a while

How sad it is

He left bruises on mother and child!

So… You Didn't Cheat

You broke my heart
You tied my hands
Every word I spoke… you took as my defeat
You walked all over my self esteem
But… you say you didn't cheat!

You took my confidence and threw it to the ground
I found out that's a way for you to hold me down
I can't look the people I pass on the street
My head is hung down
But… you say you didn't cheat!

This hurt you've caused me over the years
Has shaken my foundation
And caused me many tears
These bruises on my heart
Don't spell defeat
So… stop saying
You didn't cheat!

There are so many things worse than cheating
But… you don't seem to realize
Maybe that's the way you pretend to forget
Or maybe that's just another one of your lies
I can't begin to tell you now and I refuse to cry
But.. those wounds you left on my heart will show somehow
I'm not looking for you to apologize
And I won't except defeat

I just want you to know… it's not a big thing

If you didn't cheat!

Cheating may have been better

Because my mind would have denied

My heart would have lied

But instead you made me feel like I should have died

The love that was lost can't be regained

My heart can't hide the hurt

My mind can't erase the words that caused so much pain

All those days you treated me like dirt

I may have been a little cold

Because you never cared how much I hurt

But… you still held me down under your feet

Now stop acting like you're such a great catch

Because you say you didn't cheat!

The yelling and the breaking things

Have given you away

So… don't pretend it's all me

When I say I can't continue to stay

Love them and leave them is what I use to do

But I thought things would be different

When I decided to stay with you

So… I decided to be discreet

Honesty should have been number one

So… stop saying you didn't cheat

Look at all the horrible things you done

Now you yelling out… you didn't do nothing

So… nothing can be done!

You thought you should be treated like a king
That everything you wanted should be first on my list
But… the way you treated us everyday
Ruling with your fists
A lot of mean words were said
Tears I regularly cried
Me hiding from your anger
You not caring how hard I tried
You pushed me away when I wanted a hug
I don't know what you were thinking of
But nowhere in my world… would any of that spell LOVE!
I just wanted peace and happiness
Someone that would respect me whenever we meet
Someone I could hold close
He wouldn't ever have to say… He didn't cheat!

You keep saying you don't love me anymore
You say it all the time
Someone special could erase those bruises from my heart
And put those words out of my mind
Remember all those horrible things you done
You even called me crazy to people we would meet
So… Stop yelling at me in anger
Saying, "You Didn't Cheat"!

You're always mean to me
But nice to everyone else you meet
So… I'm not sure it really matters
If you really didn't cheat…

I'm so sorry that those awful words
You yelled at me each day
Spilled over on our children
And they can't be washed away
I'm so sorry that it ended like this
You angry all the time
But this is how it is
It's been hard for me to stay kind

All those times I was afraid to speak
You called my kindness a great defeat
So… do you still think is was a big thing
If you didn't cheat???

Women lined up at my door
While I worked everyday
Me coming home to angry fists
And me being pushed away
You said you were honest
But I was so surprised at your strife
My bank account was emptied
And those other ladies didn't know you had a wife

Now I'm tired of your anger
I don't want to be beat
Those fists of fire
Still won't make me accept defeat
Things can get better for me
Now it's becoming easier for me to speak
And I'm not sure that

YOU DIDN'T CHEAT!

Women of The Storm

They raised their children all alone

They worked in fields

You never heard them complain

They had to be strong

They were Women of the Storm!!!

They stayed in the shadows

They helped more than you know

They strived for the best

Sometimes they lingered alone

They were Women of the Storm!!!

They stood up for what they believed in

Some sat down but stayed strong

Some did things to help others even though

They were told... they were wrong

Some were beat

Some were raped

Some were hung for no wrong

They were the Women of the Storm!!!

Most stood behind men of power

Never saying a word

Giving all they had for the cause

Some just sung the most powerful songs

They were the Women of the Storm!!!

Some raised and led armies

Some were nude and still had to be strong

Some took out their enemies

Some fought their fight alone

They were the Women of the Storm!!!

Some were chained

Some were slaves

Many of them are gone

But

They showed their strength

They were the Women of the Storm!!!

Some were black

Some were white

Race don't matter

When you begin to fight

Some carried touches; then passed on

Some had their names in newspapers

And

Some were secluded and alone

They were the Great Women of the Storm!!!

Where’s MY Respect?

He walks around checking up on you
Knowing if you wanted to leave
There would be nothing he could do
He checks your trash for signs of a lie
Even though you don’t deceive him
He’s always asking you… why?
For years he acted as if you were wrong
Yelling and cursing at you
Showing his anger so strong
You haven’t done anything for him to suspect
You have always been honest
But…he still gives you no respect!

He calls you a lair and sometimes a whore
He kept saying he would leave
But he never went out that door
He knew you weren’t happy with the things he did
Saying, “I do” would’ve never happened
If you had knew it would be like this
You wouldn’t have said, “I do”
You wouldn’t have wasted your time
You wouldn’t have taken a chance
Because then marriage wasn’t on your mind
Now you’re losing sleep
Never getting enough rest
A whole lot of unwanted problems
And you are never at your best
But you won’t have to worry long
He will go somewhere

And stay gone

He will realize his mistake

Because he will never find another you

And no one will put up with the things he do

You can't understand

Your life was wrecked

And still he gives you... No Respect!

This is a dedication to the greatest poet of my time! There will never be another Maya Angelou… I thank her for sharing her most precious gift…Poetry!!!

Maya Angelou has become a great inspiration

To so many generations

That there has arisen such a great appreciation

I could never duplicate

Her works are so great

So… in my own words I dedicate

These words that I took time to create

So… that I may help regenerate

A strength in someone that will not wait

Because you have inspired my situation

By showing me the realization

That comes with faith and dedication

Now I'm reaching out to other generations

To inspire their creations

So… that there will be better future relations

Every person must know their greatness can be achieved

If they are not deceived

And they continue to believe

They must not be arrogant or show any pride

They must be glad to help others strive

So… we the people can continue to rise

We need to consider the beauty in each situation

Through independent meditation

For future generations

That she has and will inspire

So… that we will see what they desire

And greatness will be what each person requires!!!

This is dedicated to President Barack Obama

To the husband that shows compassion

To the man that sets examples

To the president that changed a nation's history

Yes, We Can...

Yes, We Did...

We Had the Audacity To Hope!!!

We have the audacity to hope

For the same treatment on the streets

That just because of our skin color

We won't be afraid of being beat...

We have the audacity to hope

For the same pay on our jobs

To be treated the same at the checkout counter

That because of our skin color we won't be robbed...

We have the audacity to hope

That president Lincoln didn't take his last ride in vain

That through his struggles for African Americans

There was something as a nation we gained...

We have the audacity to hope

That Martin Luther King's speech in our minds has not died

That through his words of wisdom

We as a nation have made great strides...

We have the audacity to hope

That through education and dedication

We have created a better nation

For our next generation...

We have the audacity to hope

That Benjamin, Marva, and President Obama have not struggled in vain
That through the years in history
The race issue has changed...
We have the audacity to hope
That this nation will get better
Because of our African American President's hope for our nation
We will start to achieve things that matter...
We have the audacity
That we have taught our children the way
To make this world a better place
As they become our leaders someday...
We have the audacity to hope
That we have come together as a people
To look after each other
To take care of those less fortunate...
To help our sisters and brothers
We have the audacity to hope
that our children learn in their schools
That our teachers are there to teach
And
That our children are not the ones that lose
WE HAVE THE AUDACITY TO HOPE!!!

A Great Poet

The passion was laid down in words
That haven't been heard before
She took all her grief and sorrow
And made it look like sorrow no more

She hid the scars so well
That no one could reveal her pain
The wounds that was left on her heart
Helped her to find strength again

Each day brings a new struggle
That open a little more of her past
Her nights of silent horror
Allows her to become steadfast

Calling out to a majority
That are unable to speak alone
Stands a great poet
Who continue to try to be strong

Bruises are covered
Scars left
Hearts closed
Despite everything else

Words unspoken
Lives destroyed again
People shaken

It never ends!

A Portrait of a Strong Woman

Her hair was curled
It hung down
In her eyes
Patience could be found
In her hands character was shown
The status she had achieved
Would surely be known
She's the portrait of a Strong Woman

She's calm most of the time
Setting her plans in motion
Thinking things through in her mind
To her... the world is a canvas
Where the paint slowly dries
She creates a better tomorrow
You can see it in her eyes
She's the portrait of a Strong Woman

To her... children are a gift
More precious than any stone
She loves and cherishes them
Her love makes them strong
Her heart is filled with lots of love
She enjoys sharing what she found
Her heart holds strength
That raises anyone up when she's around
She's the portrait of a Strong Woman

She never brags about her success

Her confidence will always show

She lifts the spirits of all she talks to

Her voice is soft yet bold

Her strength has raised many men

The power in her words… lifted them to new heights

Where they may never be again

She's the portrait of a Strong Woman

The Portrait of a Strong Woman

Is here for all to see

Here I stand having achieved greatness

Because that Strong Woman lives inside of Me!!!

I Stand Up

I stand up for the women who lost their voice
For those that were pushed aside
For those that poverty knocked down
For those that reality made hide

I stand up for the women whose eyes are closed in pain
For the ones who the world forgot their name
For the ones who were beaten down
For the ones that hung their heads in shame

I stand up for the women that has been neglected
For the ones that society rejected
For the ones that someone took their children
For the ones that's always disrespected

I stand up for the women who stand on the corner to feed their children
For the ones that hold a bottle in their hand
For the ones that have lost everything
For the ones that changed because of a man

I stand up for the women that sell their self-respect
For the ones that lay in hospital beds
For the ones on drugs
For the ones talking out of their heads

I stand up for the women that their children turn their backs on
For the ones that gave up the most

For the ones that sit quietly by
For the ones that refuse to boast

I stand up for the women that refuse to cry
For the ones that work their fingers to the bone
For the ones that never get thanked
For the ones that are usually treated wrong

I stand up for the women who's had their hearts bruised
For the ones that act as if they don't care
For the ones without nice homes
For the ones that struggle to survive anywhere

I stand up for the women that's in distress
For the ones, all over the world
For the ones that's been abused
For the ones that never had a chance to be a little girl

I stand up for the women that have lost their way
For the ones that's not strong
For the ones that still have a choice
For the ones that have gone on

I stand up for the women that have been beaten down by a man
For those that don't have control
For the ones that cry on the inside
For the ones that their hearts have grown cold

I stand up for the women who must fight to leave their house
For the ones that use make up to cover their shame

For the ones that wear dark shades to hide their black eyes

For the ones that were told they were the blame

I stand up for the women that were so deeply in love they gave up everything

For the ones that married young

For the ones that were taken down by cheaters, fists, and hurtful words

For the ones that sit and wonder… what have they done???

I stand up for the women that just gave up on life

For the ones that haven't been able to stand tall

For the ones who are willing to fight

For the ones that nobody called…

I STAND UP FOR THE WOMEN!!!

The Strength of a Woman

The strength of a Woman can be found in a child
Their loving attitude
Their heartwarming smile

The strength of a Woman can be found in a song
When you are sitting in a bar
Thinking… you're all alone

The strength of a Woman can make them move
When it seems all, they worked for is a dream
And
There is nothing they have left to lose

The strength of a Woman can be found in something she writes
A poem or a song
That brings her dreams into sight

The strength of a Woman can be found in her goal
Or
The compliment she receives
From someone that touches her soul

The strength of a Woman can be found in a word
Something wonderful she read
Or
Something great she heard

The strength of a Woman can be found in a verse

When she has been through so much

Strength is something she don't have to rehearse

The strength of a Woman can be found in her attitude

When the pressure of so many situations come down on her

She stands strong… she never thinks she should move

The strength of a Woman can be found in the creativity in her mind

When her skills become a career

The strength of a Woman can be found in her anytime

The Strength of a Woman can be found inside one's self

When she starts striving to do what she believes

And

Stop trying to please everyone else!!!

Where have you found your Strength as A Woman???

I Am A Strong Woman

Before I met you I was independent
I wasn't afraid to speak up
I didn't walk around with my head down so much
I was friendly
I smiled around everyone else
Now you want me to keep my conversation to myself
I wasn't afraid of what I had to say
And
I did something nice for someone else everyday
I was a Strong Woman!!!

I spent time with other people
I had friends that wanted me to come out
But… you want me to just sit in the house
I loved to be with my children all the time
Now you are saying only you should be on my mind
I was a Strong Woman!!!

I wanted to be someone great
Now you want to wipe that idea away
I was inspired to do so many things
My creative juices flowed like a waterfall
Now you say forget that… like it meant nothing at all
I was beautiful… inside and out
Now after listening to you
My mind is filled with doubt
I was a Strong Woman!!!

I had faith in miracles

Love was something I held dear to my heart

Now your negative attitude has torn that belief apart

I reached for heights that I hadn't before

Well, since I met you achieving don't seem easy anymore

I dreamed of a life that would show all my abilities

But since you been in my life...there's been a lot of difficulties

I was a Strong Woman!!!

So... I decided to change my plan

And

Be the Woman I know I am

I decided to create like I'm alone

Follow my dreams and make myself known

I think I'll speak to women everywhere

To let them know someone still care

Because... I was a Strong Woman!!!

I decided to spend time with my friends

And

Let them know that faith is where life begins

I decided to let them know miracles do come true

It's a miracle... I still have strength after being with here with you

I decided I can't go wrong

Letting you see that I AM STRONG

I decided you can't keep me from being heard

Because someone needs to listen to my words

I decided I'll do more giving

Because my life is worth living

I AM A STRONG WOMAN!!!

I decided to show you… I can achieve anything through the strength God gave me
I'm going to fight against all wrong
I'm letting everyone know I'm Strong
I Am A Strong Woman!!!

I won't let you destroy my mind
I won't let you continue to waste my time
You can't intimidate me anymore
It will never be like it was before
I will hold my head up all the time
Those mean words you said won't linger in my mind
I AM A STRONG WOMAN!!!

She Needs

She needs patience

Because he had none

She needs love

Because hers and his never begun!!!

She needs sweet words

Because his were always unkind

She needs to be held

Because he never had the time!!!

She needs to smile

Because with him she only cried

She needs honesty

Because he always lied!!!

She needs a gentle touch

Because his always hurt

She needs to feel special

Because to him... she was dirt!!!

She needs to sweep out the memories

Because he thought he would be back

She needs to find her strength

Because he was sure he knocked her life off track!!!

She needs to feel love

Because she never felt it from anyone before

She needs to keep her heart open

Because she deserves so much more!!!

She Enjoys

She enjoys hugs

But

He could never say

She enjoys touching

But

He always pushed her away

She enjoys conversation

But

His words were so loud

She enjoys holding hands

But

They never shared a smile

She enjoys warmth

But

He was always so cold

She enjoys sharing

But

He silenced her soul

She enjoys dancing

But

Touching wasn't his thing

She enjoys music

But

He didn't want her to sing

She enjoys walks together

But

He always said, “he was tired”

She enjoys the rainy days

Because of him… she walked alone in it and cried

She enjoys kissing

But

He always said, “No”

She enjoys having a family

But

She had to let him go!!!

I Am Beautiful

You see my hair standing all over my head
You say I should care about my size
You laugh and talk about me when I'm not there
But to your surprise
I don't care if you criticize
I know I am Beautiful!!!

You said my clothes are ugly
But
I don't want my body on display
These low-cut tops don't complement me
I wouldn't wear them anyway
But to your surprise
I don't care if you criticize
I know I am Beautiful!!!

I don't dress in the finest clothes
And
I don't get my nails done each week
You haven't seen me at my best
So just listen when I speak
But to your surprise
I don't care if you criticize
I know I am Beautiful!!!

Your hair hangs down... but it's weaved in I see
Yet your head is high up in the air

That's not what I like about me

And

When you walk, everyone turns and stare

But to your surprise

I don't care if you criticize

I know I am Beautiful!!!

Even though you may not be aware of how I feel

You may not see the look on my face

You can't always tell

What things I will embrace...

But to your surprise

I Don't Care If You Criticize

I Know...

I AM BEAUTIFUL!!!

A Dirty Word

I took off my mask
Ripped my heart off my sleeve
Dried those tears I had been crying
Because you made me believe!!!
In something I never seen
In something I never heard
Because in the world where I grew up
Love was a dirty word!!!
People would say, “I Love You”
Then they would beat you down
They would rip out your dignity
And leave you bleeding on the ground…
They put guns to your head
And say, “I’ll take your life”
Then they would say, “I Love You”
Now that wasn’t right!!!
So… I put on a mask
That would hide my sad eyes
And I struggled to live
In that dark disguise…
Like a rock on the outside
I was made of stone
But my heart was dust
In this empty world alone!!!
Then you made me believe…
In something I never seen
In something I never heard

Because in the world where I grew up
Love was a dirty word!!!
But I stood in the shadows
Of a life, I never knew
Hoping someday that I would
Find someone strong like you!!!
Sometimes people would cut you with a knife
Or leave you on the road hoping you died
Then wait for the news
So, they could act surprised!!!
They would say, "it's your fault"
You caused them to act that way
And after years of them defeating you
You believed what they had to say!!!
Then you came alone
I was so smitten I lost my breath
I couldn't help but fall in Love
In spite of myself...
So, I ripped out my heart
And laid it at your feet
You smiled, then turned, and walked away
I guess I wasn't who you expected to meet!!!
Well, I lost myself
That night under that starry sky
My heart fell... like glass on the dirt
I couldn't find my courage anymore
I had never been so hurt!!!
Then I was slapped in the face
By the things that was said to me
You were shaken by my actions

You never heard them… you didn't even see!!!

But you made me believe…

In something I never seen

In something I never heard

Because in the world where I grew up

Love was a dirty word!!!

So… all my life I hid my heart

I kept it locked in chains

So, no one could touch it

And I couldn't feel any pain!!!

But I still tried to stand

With my head held high

But every plan I had felled

And all I could do was cry!!!

My heart was crushed

And I was shaking my head

Wondering what was I thinking

You never meant anything you said!!!

In your voice, there was a difference

That I heard right away

You spoke with such assurance

You put me at ease that day…

My dreams all came rushing back

I could feel my heart beat once more

But soon it was all a dream

Because I ended up crying on the floor!!!

Still I believed…

In something I never seen

In something I never heard

Because in the world where I grew up

Love was a dirty word!!!

Because Love caused hurt

And Love caused pain

It left you struggling

To hide your shame!!!

Oh, my goodness… it was all a joke

That you played on me too

I thought you were different

So… I really trusted you!!!

Then you hit my heart so hard

I knew I was deceived

Love is A Dirty Word!

I don't know why I ever believed!!!

Now I stand in awe

Because I was deceived

But still I remember

Once you made me believe…

In something I never seen

In something I never heard

Because in the world where I grew up

Love was A Dirty Word!!!

LOVE IS A DIRTY WORD!!!

Blank Space

For years, she sat in silence
No reactions to the violence
That happened from day to day…
Everyone was whispering
But no one was listening
To what she had to say…

Her pillow is wet with tears
Yet she hides her fears
So, no one would even know…
That the things she had seen
Haunted her dreams
As she tried to let them go…

Sarcasm became her shield
For the walls, she had to build
Around her wounded heart…
Just when she started to forget
There was another hit
This one tore her apart…

Being bruised as a child
Had taken away her inner smile
And left her soul covered in grey…
So many people were there
That pretended to care
But never understood her anyway…

For years, she sat quiet
Even though inside there was a riot
Voices screaming, she wasn't ok…
Just when she thought she had conquered it
Her heart took another hit
That left her life turned a different way…

She was vulnerable and kind
It was mistaken for weakness in everyone else's mind
Now she was left to drown…
No one to lean on for support wasn't her choice
It had become part of her life by force
Now she had to turn it all around…

Can a heart that once beat well
Rise from such a horrible tale
To seek a dream once more…
Or will the silence she once embraced
Be the bitterness she forever tastes
As it had been so many times before!

Her Strength

She was beaten
She was dragged
She bleeds tears where she lay…
She was kicked
She was stomped
By night and day!
Her children watched from a distance
Unable to help anyone else
She smiled at them through her tears…
She always got up
In spite of her health
Always hiding her fears!
She would gently raise a hand
Put a finger to her lips
“No more tears” she would mouth…
She always stood up for her children
Her body was weakened from the beatings
That was known without a doubt!
The fear she hid to protect their hearts
They could only see her strength
She would not let domination be his gain…
The moments he was gone… they cherished
Each night he returned
To inflict physical and emotional pain!
Now in the light day
The house is silent and she’s alone
Her strength is what her children will recall…
She was chained in fear

Covered in bruises

But she didn't take the last fall!

She protected her children

It was worth all the pain she endured

Her days will never be the same…

She sits and wonders

Why she stayed so long

Now she tries to hide her shame!

Her darkened shades

And visible limp

Reminds her all too well…

The wounds that can't be seen

Hidden from the world

Makes her story hard to tell!

Domestic Violence (part 1)

It started out with words
That seemed a little strange
We acted like it was ok
That changed everything…
Discussions became arguments
A little more each day
Little things became huge
Who knew it would be that way???
Then you started yelling
Each time you talked at me
I couldn't really explain it
But you even looked differently!!!
I begin to worry all the time
I wasn't sure I would survive
So… each day I tried to escape
The stranger you became inside…
I didn't know this would happen
Or that you would start to act this way
Now I'm wondering when will we get to the place
Where we don't have to say…
Domestic Violence took another life today!!!

Now objects are thrown in every direction
Broken glass is across the floor
Fists flying through walls
We can't live this way anymore…
Windows are broken

Shot are fired by your hand

Lives are destroyed

In a motionless desire from a careless man...

Words are spoken in anger

Many hurtful days were in store

Living a life in fear

Is worse than it was before...

Flashbacks start to happen

Memories from a broken child

Another household unraveling

In such a short while...

You begin to worry all the time

Will your family survive?

Each day a new plan of escape

The stranger your dad became inside!!!

You were too young to remember

Or to know he acted those ways

Now you're just thankful

That Domestic Violence didn't take all your lives those days!!!

Tears are forever falling

Around so many hearts that's been bruised

Lives were touched and torn apart

Something you would never choose...

Now you sit and wonder

How did you end up here?

A mirror image of your youth

Everything seems so unclear...

Just thinking about when you first met

He seemed so nice and kind

You had no way of knowing

That he would become a stranger with time!!!

Now with tear filled eyes you sit and wonder

If you and your children will survive

You must find the strength to fight

The stranger he becomes inside!!!

Domestic Violence (part 2)

You couldn't have known this would happen
You couldn't have known he would be this way
But you are truly thankful
That Domestic Violence didn't claim all your lives that day...
Sometimes children are left without their parents
Fathers and mothers lining the walls of the jails
Horrible things happening behind closed doors
Women always too ashamed to tell...
Stories on the news
That show the final tale
No one can imagine how hard it is
For the ones that live and survive this hell...
Sometimes the pain goes too deep
Because of the fear, you hold inside
Not enough people are willing to stand up
For those of us that want to survive...
You never know what goes on in the shadows
When the doors are close and the curtains pulled down
How he acts on the outside
Is totally different when no one else is around...
It's so important that you don't blame yourself
You couldn't have changed the way he was at all
The day your life started to change
Is something you will forever recall...
Now you sit shaking your head
Just wondering how you survived
Years of that unbelievable anger
From the stranger... he became inside!!!

Several times you made plans

Positive you could get away

Somehow, he always found out

You stayed...

wondering would Domestic Violence claim your life that day...

Now there's memories you can't shake

Sometimes they still rattle you deep down inside

But you are strong and determined

To find the strength to survive...

This will continuously be a part of your life

From now until the end of time

Even though your heart carries many scars

Your future this will not define!!!

Love will come

Just don't be afraid to try again

Someone will treasure your beauty

And you will want good things to begin...

Now push your worrying away

Be thankful that you did survive

He will no longer be your concern

Or... The Stranger He Became Inside!!!

As a nation... we will get to the point

That we won't have to say

Domestic Violence is being overcame

It hasn't taken any lives today!!!

The List

When you are angry at me… Hug me, and kiss me

Then tell me it's going to be fine

When you want to throw something… Throw your arms around me

When you want to say something mean to me… Mean it when you say, "I Love You"

When you decide, you have had enough… Give me thirty days to change your mind

When you feel like giving me a piece of your mind… Let it be covered with your heart

When you want to yell at me… Sang me a song loudly

When you want to call me a name… Call me beautiful!!!

When you want to mention my weight… Say you can't wait to be alone with me

When you want to hit me… Hit me with some words that will take my breath away

When you want to make me cry… Make me cry out "Baby I Love You"

When you want to hurt me… Hurt me by holding me tightly in your strong arms

When you say I'm crazy… Say I'm crazy about you

When you want to turn something on me…Turn me on with something you say

When you want to put your hands in my hair… Run your hands through it

When you want to put your hands on me… Touch me gently enough so I will enjoy it

When you want to threaten me… Threaten to try and make me Love you more

When you want to give me an ultimate choice… give me the choice to Love you longer or make you happier

If you ever think I'm cheating… Know that I can only cheat myself out of a deeper Love affair with you

If I let you down… Let me be letting you down gently on our bed

When I disappoint you… Let me be dismissing a point that wasn't that important anyway

If you ever lose faith or you ever lose trust…There will be a problem… because there will be no more us!!!

If you want to lose something… Lose yourself in my gaze

If you ever want to play me… Play me a love song that makes me think of only you

When you want to hold on to something… Hold on to my hand

When you want to break something… Break the barriers that keep us from sharing our deepest secrets with each other

When you want to make me do something... Make Me LOVE You More!!!

When you say you Love me... Show me (with as many hugs and kisses as you want to)

When you look at me... Look in my eyes

When you want to feel something...Feel the chemistry between us

When you want to hold me... Hold me above all else except GOD

When we are together... Make me feel like I'm the only person in the world

When you wonder... Wonder how you can make me happier

When you kiss me... Kiss me like you're connecting our hearts

When you speak to me... Say the words softly so they can touch my spirit

If you ever want to push me... Let it be a push to my ego or my self esteem

A push that will send me far above all doubt and discouragement

If you ever want to go ... Then go the extra mile to Love me like no one has ever done before

If you ever want to remember something... Remember the day we met and how you felt when you first looked in my eyes

If you ever want to leave... Then leave me wanting to spend more time loving you!!!

www.ingramcontent.com/pod-product-compliance
Ingram Content Group UK Ltd.
Pitfield, Milton Keynes, MK11 3LW, UK
UKHW051137260726
13967UKWH00010B/3100

9 780359 736072